CW00689664

Natural and other Musings

Miranda Cox

Edward Gaskell
DEVON

First published 2008
Edward Gaskell publishers
Old Sawmill
Grange Road
Bideford
Devon EX39 4AS

isbn   (10) 1 -898546 -99 -1
isbn   (13) 978 -1 -898546 -99 -3

©Miranda Cox

Natural and other Musings
Miranda Cox

All rights reserved. No part of this publication may be reproduced, stored in a
retrieval system, or transmitted in any form by any means electronic, mechani-
cal, photocopying, scanning, recording or otherwise, without the prior written
permission of the publishers.

Typeset, printed and bound by
Lazarus Press
Caddsdown Business Park
Bideford
Devon
EX39 3DX
www.lazaruspress.com

	page		page
In Cornwall	5	Leaving	32
Filled with Nature	6	Walls	32
Flu	7	Stepping on Moonlight	33
Haiku	7	Autumn and Musing	34
Old Cypress	8	Shut Out	34
Formal Moon	8	Haiku	35
Stay the Hand	9	Untidy Poem	35
A Shy Person	10	Bad	36
From the Buddha	11	Dentist	37
Sweetie	11	Song of Earth	38
Doing the Right Thing	12	Stares	39
Man's Right Leg	12	Going Ahead	40
Feminist Biblery	14	Angry Tree	41
Lost	15	Northam Burrows	42
Old Grief	16	Furies	42
Cobwebs	17	Autumn Leaves	43
Slow	17	Gloucester Cathedral	43
The Web	18	Canvassing	44
Waking-Sleeping	18	Now-ness	45
Picking up the Pieces	19	Motions from the Floor	46
Which is Real?	20	Humanist Geometry	48
Pembrokeshire Cliff Walk	21	Blossom Stars	48
Can't Stop	22	Pink and White	49
Pembrokeshire	23	Belle Bouteille	49
Wordless	24	Longggg Meetingggg	50
Through	25	Meeting My Aunt	51
Cat	26	No Supplications	52
Spring is Sprung	27	Curves	53
Rain	27	Tea With a Walnut Tree	53
The Old Tree	28	Nun	54
Polite	29	Wind From My Sails	55
Birth Book	31	Sinking of the Teabag	56

To Nature

IN CORNWALL

Unravelling tears of vulnerable blue
drop deep where the
salty sea laps at my soul.

moss climbs up stone walls
and whorls of lichen linger
in a green and ancient way
on standing stones

I lie spreadeagled on the the moor
by a murmuring stream
and float upwards with the pure notes
of a skylark

the rusty ruins of tin mines
bang in the wind
as if calling to ghostly workers.

peering over cliff edges I watch
boundless waves, horsing over rocks,
rear towards cracks where kittiwakes
fly in circumspect circles

and stretching over it all -
the vast canopy of sky
sketching outline of sheep and bent tree,
curving round harbours of bobbing boats,
till it swoops off
to meet the horizon
and kiss the ocean
with a smudge of rain.

FILLED WITH NATURE

I am so filled with nature
That branches grow
Through my body
Turning into hair twigs
And poking leaves
Through crevices of skin.

Tendrils wrap lightly around veins
And draw sap into my heart
Which sings like a lark
And pumps music
To the rythmic tide of spinal seas.

My feet of earth support trunk-like legs
And my hands fly
Through low sky
Sketching arcs of dialogue

In my dreams sundials tick,
I lose edges,
Suck in oceans of salty water
And spray fountains of whirring worlds

FLU

Noises carve shapes on my body
breath is a harsh embrace
the world muted lies
with reality an elusive
white shadow

headaching tenderness
with every move,
I fall into a shifty sleep
which only promises
feverish dreams

longing for cooling potions
and healing touch
when will the swaying stop
and life take me firmly
in its grasp again ?

HAIKU

Raindrop falls on leaf
Licks it wetly stem to tip
And falls still kissing

OLD CYPRESS
(at Tregwainton Gardens, Cornwall)

The taste of a tree
licked by shade
pungent and woody.

Ripples of bark and
twisting arms reach
to greet the sky
splicing through a
canopy crown
of woven twigs.

Shafts of light
pierce dark crevices
while unseen roots
spread a labyrinth underground
clawing into the granite
to stay this great majesty.

FORMAL MOON

The moon is formal tonight
she sails stiffly across the black sky
cutting through clouds with a
sharp crescent edge.

A fine silver sliver,
stars shrink at her approach
the wind cannot touch her
she's in her element -
riding high -
yet secretly she hopes
the sun will never let her down.

STAY THE HAND

Round the edges and into the middle
Weeds speed grow
Pushing roots deep
They shout, "me, me, me"
To the sky
And scatter seed in a rush
Knowing there's safety in numbers.

They look with scorn
On the nurtured babies - lettuce and carrot
With fancy names like little gem and early nantes
Fondled into germination with plant food and pots,
Pricked out and prettified in cultivated soil

And when you're not looking they crowd in
Harbouring slugs and snails
And aiming invisible kicks
At the little darlings

But before wholesale slaughter is delivered
Stay the weeding hand that says,
"No, out you come."
And consider
the sunny dandelion with her fairy clock
sustains the liver
-borage bright, blue and starshaped
is loved by bees
thistle with her purple spike gives food for birds
and that old stinger nettle rots into the best compost.

So maybe there's a middle way - don't cull all
let nature sprawl with her rich diversity
and enjoy the fruits of less labour.

A SHY PERSON STRUGGLES WITH THE DIN AT DINNER

All around
gabbling mouths
dribbling words
puddles of slimy ego
congeal on dinner plates

inside her tongue tied shyness
thoughts scramble into scabs of fear
and her throat is frozen with the debris
of stagnant memories

she watches the lips labouring
like so many fish hemmed in a tank
sucking at the side in futile
longing for the ocean

then she lubricates her own tank
with a bottle of wine
and watches a flounder unfurl
into a shark
cracking the glass
with precision pronouncements
snapping at sloppy sentences with sword teeth

the gobblers gradually grind to a gape
eyes round and glassy
they press back helplessly
as unleashed torrents spew over them

FROM THE BUDDHA

From the Buddha I'm learning
to notice the arrows coming towards me
and turn them into lotus blossoms,
to notice the arrows coming from me
and turn them into lotus blossoms.
All the disturbing, attacking, averting mind games -
turn them into lotus blossoms
on and on
an infinite practice.
No-one is better or worse than me.
Nothing affects me that I don't have
Feelers foraging for already.
I am not wrong or right.
Let others have their propensities –
Understand it as their path, their search
we are all lotus blossoms
growing out of the mud to great beauty
deep pink lotus blossoms softening into
the gentle pulsing heart of the universe.

SWEETIE

You whispered sweet nothings
chocolate somethings
caramel everythings
into my ear and
all over my hair,
sticky everywhere
took ages to wash out
next time, honey,
please whisper
savoury nothings

DOING THE RIGHT THING

I'm never doing the right thing
because I'm always doing the wrong thing
if the right thing looked me in the face
or shouted "hello I'm over here
I'm the right thing come and do me"
if I did it
it would become the wrong thing
because I was doing it.
So the only way round it
is to know
that whenever I'm doing anything
which is the wrong thing
because I'm doing it
it must be the right thing
because it's wrong
and that's what
I'm meant to be doing.

MAN'S RIGHT LEG IN AN ART EXHIBITION

Yes, this is me, right leg
sticking out of t' wall
from calf downwards :
bit of black trouser
bit of black on white
hairs on flesh
black lace up shoe
walked a long way I have
half of sixteen thousand miles
- or thereabouts I reckon
and cycled a good many an' all.
In me latter years I pumped an
accelerator and brake fervently

and then, dammit it all,
I get stuck in the snow in 1963
bitter cold winter that one
Well, nobody found me for ages,
I didn't warm up quick enough
frozen turns to gangrene
and before I know it
I'm off, Cut, Amputated !
Without so much as a "thank you"
for all my years of service
and I end up here in a bloody art gallery.
You should try taking the shoe and sock off
If you really want to see something

black it was,
black, purple and yellow
and putrid – stank like hell
now I'm petrified, sprayed with something
too well preserved, me,
can't even rot in hell, let alone peace,
well how'd you like it ?
It's not natural – being here
I might run –or hop off soon
you'll see, or not,
I've been scraping round the edges
pulling away from the wall
when no-one's looking
I'll be away
so ta –ra oh, and by the way
my name's Bill,
the left one was called Mary
wonder what happened to her?

FEMINIST BIBLERY

Burneth thou thy
uninvented brassiere
in the BC years.
That fearsome, gruesome god
producteth verily from
churly chauvinism and
postulating patriarchy.
Returneth thou to
thy matrilinear matrices
and mingle thy menses into
pungent unguents to
pusueth thy ends.
Raise thou thy sons
to respecteth well
thine female principle.
Thy husbands may be truly afeared
of their male god's wrath
but a crack on their polish-ed pate
with thy burnish-ed cooking vessel
will bringeth them down to
thy mother eartheth
with a big bumpeth.

LOST

I can't
find the trees
green glimpses
grief with leaves
tear-shaped,
branching out;
or would I
lose sight falling
sliding down
a wall of sadness.

Where are you?

Where am I?

long ago,
the birds sing,
I disappeared,
high up,
took your needs,
digested whole,
for mine
please see me
I've forgotten
I'm forgotten
the plants grow
I water them,
take care of me
I never fledged.

OLD GRIEF

Sobs rising and falling
throb and ebb
of long held grief
like centuries of river tides.

Spilling down my cheeks
estuaries lapping
water sighing, welling,
spinning in pools
rushing down a scramble of rocks
and smooth into the shallows

like driftwood I
float seawards
to arrive
salty and sodden
and sink at last into her
welcoming waves.

COBWEBS

I like the way cobwebs
straddle a room
insinuating curves
across an angular ceiling,
defying gravity and
insisting their existence
out of reach.

Dieting spiders whom I rarely see
have a peck of fly
occasionally
but really seem to dine
on nothing but time.
Methinks I have no right
To bring them down to earth
Floored by a broom
Let them trapeze their life aloft
While I scrape by below

SLOW

carp lazily
brown and smooth
pebbling in motes of
faded dusty sunshine;
old summer
trails dry leaves and
the current stretches green
dawdling fronds
mmm... water soothes
gently shadows lengthen

THE WEB

Planet spins
and the web is woven
threads of orange patterned leaves,
green brown shadowed forests
lichen light and rain dripping

Suffuse sepia tints
the old days
rolling on over into midnight blue
and pale dawn,
swallows swoop
and sparrows chatter a backdrop
humans fall into grace
then lose it in words
snarled out of connection
from thorny thoughts
and blown into disastrous deeds
the climate shifts, the earth cries
- everything waits on now.

WAKING-SLEEPING

I wake a drop
dreams tease
fear is empty
days land on days
a prairie of time
sliding into night
grass grows tall as my mind
spangled with
dandelions, lily tigers
prowling through
stalking prey
of nightmares
we gallop away
and stumble into dark slumber.

PICKING UP THE PIECES

There they were on the floor
the pieces – because you'd
walked out the door
too many to pick
up all at once
tears aren't glue
and they would misfit
your presence having leaked away.

So I began apiece
a new lease
(how much - 5, 10 years?)
of life, being after all stuck with it.
Some segments became
a careful, growing delight
combed from collapse
to spin like dewdrops
and glitter with recovery
but some clumps were
of leaden mood
resentful clinker
mulled fear mined out of future pitfalls.

No golden horizons
greeted the mountainous struggle
but I came to a
sense that the bits
can fit into certain wholes
and pieces, once picked
up and handled,
gather a resolute stickiness.

WHICH IS REAL?

I'm caught in seriousness
like a buzzing fly
wrapped over and over
with fine spider filigree.
Trapped by desperate thoughts –
something's wrong,
disapproval lurks,
invasion threatens,
boundaries shiver,
muscles ready for flight or fight
worry weaves its lines
into my face.

then I look up
and see the blue sky,
fluffy clouds,
hear a robin sing
watch sunshine play
on whispering leaves
then a passing shower sends
diamond drops of rain
plopping into puddles
life becomes beautiful.

And I wonder
Which is real?

PEMBROKESHIRE CLIFF WALK

The cliff walk passes
-strong stoned underfoot -
by giddy drops
looking down to the dashing sea
which stopped short by mocking rocks
spits white foam
then smoulders in sullen sway.

Splashes of autumn fern
orange against green turfed tops
weave back and forth like our steps
from inlet to headland crag
till a stone circle on an emerald hill
looms out of ancient time.

We sit on a rough hewn bench and gaze
at the grey granite beach below
strewn with slate and boulder
and sliced in two by a stream
then stumble duskwards
the pale path lit by a rounding moon

CAN'T STOP

Words twisting into shape
and running full charge
[shadows of lurking behind]
 I can't stop
their buzzing race
mindlessly filling spaces
in case oh no
I might not exist
If there's emptiness

let me spin
and web myself
enough fibres
for a body
full pelt of knowledge
past present
future headed
legging it full throttle
I scream ME
alive before death
at least
the human race won
but lost as tomorrow's expectations
press down
and my mind is
pushed into busy-ness

PEMBROKESHIRE

Glossy black feathered rooks
on Pembroke telegraph wires
caw hum
in the white beak sunshine.

Stones trip down
autumn paths
along the boulder brooking rush
of yesterdays rain

Winter hovers
In the slashing wind.

I'm drawn to endings,
Thinking of death:
Plant my body
for rich earth
round an acorn
when I die
so in the spring
I may sustain life still,
With a fizz of energy
and glow green in the airy sky
while my sweet decay is hugged by knotty roots.

WORDLESS

At the party people prowl
stale with pretence and
sherry rotted words
smiles grip their faces
covering curved, bladed lips
throats gag on unspat venom.

I slither out through the slats
blinding a window
-too much snake talk
leaves me wordless.

Outside the air is
wet and alive
raindrops shiver
and I slice dance
with eddies of leaves
windwoven in cloud light
then drift home to empty rooms,
and the simple pleasure
of a purring cat as she settles
on my lap.

THROUGH

I'm at a place where
tears fall
shiver soft -
a veil has dropped
grazing the edges
I reach through -

and want to sob
a river running;
two dimensions
touch so lightly
my soul wobbles
sipping life

I've been searching
 in the wrong places
- avoiding this because
of the beautiful fragile pain
and the fear of no-one else
coming

outside the rain runs off the tarmac
to meet the wide-armed earth.

CAT

Black streak of cat
through a crack of door
leapt upstairs
lurked round the corner
to spring playfully
and make a mad dash
for the bedroom.

Breathless I arrive
to find all innocence
eyeing me lazily,
curled up
nose tucked
whiskers soft
and snuggled

Puss, I love the cosiness
of your company
on a cold winter's night
and morning purr with
velvet paws
but when summer comes
and fleas breed
I'm afraid no furry temptation
will melt my aversion
to itchy bites in the night.

SPRING IS SPRUNG

Spring is sprung
through a mattress
thrown out to grass.
Green stalks through
rusted mortal coils,
insects revel in rot,
birds pluck at stuffing
to feather nests and
gradually, as moss
spreads its spongy feet
and little plants wriggle rooting around,
grasping a springboard for shoots
with petals at the ready,
a flowerbed of sorts
is born.

RAIN

I saw it sweep across the sky
a bruise of clouds
a grey shoulder
hard tears stinging the sea
then gone
leaving behind
the cool blue gaze
of a winter sky

THE OLD TREE

The old tree
wiles away a century
watching the world
with gnarled wisdom.
Turning slowly to check
its woody body
its beetle eye spies
a orange stain spreading
with fungal smile
across the cracking bark
and with mossy thought
drops the rotting branch
to forest floor.

In a dark wet fold
he tends a young fern
soft spiral green
finding foot
in scraps of leaf mould.

High, high up
twigs mingle with sky,
birds sing of their home
and curving leaves
draw their love from light.

As seasons turn towards autumn
the acorns ripen
in fairy cups
and he's ready
when the wind comes
to scatter his seed
far and wide
in the hope of
growing more gnarled wisdom
to give silent witness
to a struggling world.

POLITE

After you
No after you
Oh thank you
You're very welcome
Please sit down, would you like a cup of tea?
Well if it's not too much trouble
Of course not
That's so kind of you
Milk, sugar, lemon, weak, strong, medium, mug, cup and saucer?
Er milk, no sugar, medium, mug
A medium mug?
No medium strong, any old mug, I mean a mug would be just right
Yes, I don't have old mugs
Oh no, of course not
Earl grey, lapsang souchong, darjeeling?
Earl grey please I love that bergamot flavour - smell - which is it?
Scone, teacake, cucumber sandwich?
How generous, what a wonderful choice, er scone please
Plain, wholemeal, sultana?
Oh sultana is very nice isn't it?
Cream, butter, jam?
Just butter please

Shortbread, fruitcake, madeleine?
Well a slice of fruitcake would be delicious
Raisin and cherry, walnut and brandy, apple and apricot?
Gosh, ohhh - apple and apricot, I haven't tried that kind,
you must be a brilliant cook
Thick, medium or thin slice?
Well, thin please, got to watch my figure haha, really I bet you have
a wonderful kitchen, all homely, aga, cat on a rocking chair. . .
Not really, I'm allergic to cats and I buy it all from the grocers
make yourself at home while I nip out
Ooohhhhh you don't have to bother
It's no bother at all, - read a magazine - Good Housekeeping,
Cordon Bleu Cookery, Devon Life
You're too kind, really too kind, I'll just sit here then - oh she's gone.
I don't think I'll stay, it feels a bit strange, I'll just slip out, shall I
leave a tip? Yes, no, yes - quick. . .

BIRTH BOOK

Not having children
I decided to write a baby
nine months of words coursing
through rich veins.

I took lit vits and did yogic arsanas* –
sitting for days on my backside
with deep inhalations of paragraphs.
I chased my pen from line to page,
flicks of ink racing
my hand grew fit and lean
the rest of me, well, lumbered.

Then I hit a wall within view
of the last chapter and collapsed against
twenty feet of mental bricks and mortar,
So I took my body for a walk
- oh to smell the sparkling air
and see green views.

Refreshed I returned
And went into labour
Twelve hard hours later
A book was born
Weighing in at 33,000 words
A petite novella
Full of vibrancy,
A joy to hold,
Once printed, stapled and covered
I kissed it, placed it tenderly in a
Big squishy envelope
And posted it by stork mail
To my publisher.

*asanas are yogic postures

LEAVING
[from a picture]

He's moving - blurred
and the landscape – still
holds him.
The gate shows a way
will he spin through
And only his soft footprint
in the dew
left to prove his place
and say
"I was here once."

WALLS

You slap me with a wall of words
I can't slip one vowel
Into the mix
However much I lever
With my tongue trowel
At the bricks –sideways, edgeways
I open my mouth to try
But there are no cracks
And verbal concrete smacks
Me in the face
So I retreat to a place
Of outward compliance
While inside I build
A wall of silence.

STEPPING ON MOONLIGHT

1

Through the landing window
moon sloped in
showing off her near fullness
In a white puddle on the carpet.

In a dark mood
I stamped on her
But she had an irritating habit
Of re-appearing
every time I moved on
so I abandoned her
to be faded by morning
and went off to bathe in my own puddle,
adding lavender for purpleness.

2

moon sloped in
through landing window
and pooled lightly
on the carpet
in a dark mood
I stamped on her
but she shone on
beyond pale
so I swam into
Her luminosity

AUTUMN AND MUSING ON THE CANAL

Mind sluicing the canal
sifting losses and reflections
mallards sail smoothly past
green sheen heads aloft
silhouettes to a blue sky.

Clarity cuts deep
old wounds bleed
sharp tears

Trees undress,
their leaves
linger on the water
dipping into the stillness
as shadows ripple under
an ancient brick bridge.

SHUT OUT

They saw her
shutting out the angel of the mind
crushing his wings
with curdled music
and pebbles of mottled word
his faded fall
left pink notes hanging
like soft blossom
but she was blinded by
ice drop splinters of
sharp edges of pain
dulled his cry
and they could do nothing
for the door was closed.

HAIKU

George you're such a Bush
Have you ever hugged a tree?
Go and do it now.

UNTIDY POEM written in Portugal

This poem could be neater
But a bee-eater
Caught my eye in a flash of colour.
As I turned to watch
The pen made a dash
Across the page
Dragging my hand
In unthinking scrawl
Ink flowing everywhere
While up in the endless sky
Bright blue and copper feathered glowing
And dipping
And my sight blessed
And the pen came to rest
Here.

BAD

I am a sweet little foot
Stamping on a daisy, an ant,
My brother's finger
Then waiting to see
What happens next -
There is death
And I did it
Here is screaming
Which brings mummy running
But I never did it
I'm drawing in my book
And babies can't talk.

And now lying in the dark
I know I'm bad
And the monsters will get me

DENTIST

"Open wide"
But my jaw won't stretch
"Mmmmmmmmmmm"
aaahhhhhhhhhh
"upper right fifth
yes big hole here"
please no drilling
not too deep
watch out for my brain
ohhh the pain
oh it's over
no it's not
the rumbling machine
I'm not a road
my teeth aren't tarmac
"right on track
nearly there
now the filling
now bite gently"
I'll bite your finger off
"how's that feel?
fine
good
rinse
[spit]
there we are
wasn't so bad
here's
the bill -"

SONG OF EARTH

Song of earth
Singing singing singing singing
A coloured catch of cries
Crying crying crying crying
Hum of earth humming
Call of earth calling

Poetry of earth
In light and dark shadow
A million sighs of wind
Circling the globe
A million shades of green
Planting their roots in her

And where were we
When she began her verse
She who creaks a little now
She who is thirsty and waiting

The poetry of earth
Fading fading fading fading
Fear of earth
dying dying dying dying

STARES [at a different-shaped body]

You might not realise
but when my hand catches your eyes
I curl up inside
cos you go right through my skin
though I haven't asked you in

so many people stare
and then just look away
what have I done to feel so shunned
how would you fare if you were there
please look up and see
that in here - it's me.

GOING AHEAD

If you've lost parts that were held dear
I hope you'll draw a drop of cheer
From this tale I want to tell
cos at the end it does end well:

Bits of me have gone ahead
To see what it's like to be dead
Teeth and nails and lots of hair
Those have gone without a care
But the part that's gone furthest in physical time
Is my right foot cut off when in its prime
It wasn't right the doctors related
And so they went and amputated

It's been gone quite a while
And I'm waiting to hear
What it's like to exist
without form or career
one thing I've thought
 and would like to mention
- in bits that have gone
there'll be much less tension-
and these are the facts
that I think to be true
at least it's relaxed
after all it's been through.

ANGRY TREE

I'm a hunting tree
With whipping limbs
I'll snatch you with snarling roots
And throw you to the underdogs

I'll curse your saws,
And blunt their bloody teeth
And cut you down as you would me
I'll leave you stumped
With stupidity

You've had your chance
Now take the blame
You've put the human race to shame
Your greed for cash has made you a fool

And those who can't see
The trees for the wood
Will make good compost
Understood?

NORTHAM BURROWS

Sheep laze on the burrows
They graze on the furrowed brows
Browsing on the common grass
Musing on the dunes
Nibbling stubbled blades
Near pebbleridge or
On pimpley bridge
All praise for the days of
Summer past long lasting
Long tasting the sweet chewing
The early morning dew
Long may all the rare plants grow
And sow their seeds in soil of salt marsh
And blow in sea winds

FURIES

Aye a poem of furies
Spitting at the slow cud munching
Of men's minds
Their damp clodded thoughts
Full of numb fears
So any new ideas fester
Faster than a blade of grass
Cut so short by lawn mower madness
That it's grown brown
The green having leaked away.

AUTUMN LEAVES

Leaves, unfaithful to green,
try out new colours
and clothed in orange and yellow
wave in the wind
Shouting 'look at me, look at me!'
Until they break from their branch
and leap into the sky
soaring silently for a second
in translucent blueness
then twirling in a final dance
down to the ground
where with a crimson smile
they die.

GLOUCESTER CATHEDRAL FROM THE TRAIN

Across a sea of choppy grey roofs
The sturdy square tower
Of the cathedral
Shoves its chin into the blue sky
God's not up there mate
Nor heaven neither
I say
But it ignores me
With centuries of righteous indifference

CANVASSING

Knocking on doors
With a ready smile
They open like vents,
I step backwards
As people appear to pour
Pent-up anti-political rancour
From long furred-up mouths
Unplumbing unknown depths
Hammering anvils of anger.
I make a quick sidestep
to avoid this avid rage which
spurts over my shoulder
onto nicely mown grass.

I hurry on to
Froth with friendliness
further along the street
Stroking babies and old ladies
Kissing dogs and cats
I think I'm going bats. . .
I rein myself in
And rain blurs my lists
And I lean against door frames
And nod like I've never nodded before
So tired I long to lie on the floors
Of porches and conservatories
But no, don't conserve a tory

So I teeter on
Now nodding to myself
About bin bags and dog mess
And litter, louts and looters.
It gets later and my gait falters
So I let my cycle take me home
Hanging on to handlebars
As the pedals circle my feet
Reaching the front door
I pour myself in to ponder
Upon this democracy thing.

NOW-NESS

I had a flash of now-ness
But it didn't last
Alas I must lament
It went into the past -

MOTIONS FROM THE FLOOR

Motions from the floor
The arm-chair called for
preening its pretty cover skin
With the beginnings of a grin
It waited for reply
But none were very nigh
Though the carpet
Bagged a brief attention
For its dotty intervention
suggesting any e-motions
Yes I'll go for sadness, joy
And a brief bout of fury
Called the clerk to the jury
So we duly expressed
What is usually repressed
Though we knew not why

Pro-motions and de-motions
Passed quickly by
When the only voter
Was clearly a fly

What about undulating motions?
Questioned a quirky quipper flipper
Who was really a whale
Dressed up in sail
Then sea came in over pebbleridge
(It was the temperature of a fridge)
and rendered us motionless
in a turquoise ocean
only our ears bobbing in the breeze
till one councillor began to sneeze
and waterlogged we sank.

- our smell was rather rank -
to become nibbles for fishes
indeed such tasty dishes.

Once our souls were freed
we rose to heaven
(I think it was nearly half past seven)
where God was holding a meeting
and Raphael did a fly by and
asked for
motions from the sky
some of us fell
to hell
where satan said
I've just had a motion
In my compost loo
Any of you want to go too?
We all politely declined
Which wasn't very kind
But the devil chose to ignore
- he was sucking on some gore-
and said you can stuff meetings
just turn up the heating
and tell of bad things done
so I can have some fun
and entice the un-nice
To visit - I'm feeling acquisitive
At this point I woke up with a nudge
The planners had judged
In a developer's favour again
So I went insane
And have stayed that way
To this very day. . .

HUMANISTIC GEOMETRY

But where asked the square?
I'm coming round said the circle
I feel like I don't oblong,
sighed the rectangle
it's all so one-sided, moaned the line
you just don't try angled the isosceles

It all got a bit protracted
and they started yawning by degrees
so the oval suggested a tiny bedtime drink
and went horizontal.
They multi-laterally agreed
except the line
which decided to stay up.

BLOSSOM STARS

Blossom has fallen on the ground
like stars to an inverted sky
constellation clusters of lilac
lie strewn on the path
before me.
I am walking in heaven
surrounded by perfume
feet float through clouds
and my head tilts round
in a meeting circle

PINK AND WHITE

There's a girl on the train
in a pink and white dress
she's eating a pink and white sweet
she's so neat
even her feet
wear pink and white sandals
she's a strawberry delight
I might just lean across
And take a small bite

BELLE BOUTEILLE

La belle bouteille vert
Sur la mur
Se reflete la lumiere du soleil
Et reste la pendant longtemps -
Dans l'automne, l'hiver au printemps
Et puis un jour
Une autre belle bouteille est arrivee
Et s'assit sur la mur aussi
Quelle belles les deux
Vieux bouteilles vert.
Mais dans l'ete
Se jete un roc
Et smashe au smithereens
Les belles bouteille greens.

LONGGGG MEETINGGGG

At 7pm the members sat upright at their seats
The radiators poured excessive heat
We started on the first item
It soon dragged its words
and slurred to a drone
beads of sweat on its brow
the chair chugged onto number two
and to many the view of how we'd reach number three
gained appeal as we began to veer and list somewhat
slumping in our clammy seats
till twas quite forgot
why we were there
though the chair sallied on
with an upward beat -
like the prow of a boat
sailing along through salty spray
she had her say again and again
foaming at the agenda
though one by one
one member would tender
an apology and leave
until we all were gone.

MEETING MY AUNT

Her eyes peer out
Beneath a hat of bedraggled straw.
Broken stems droop over sunstained cheeks
And under an aquiline nose
Her mouth stretches like
Two tadpoles tete a tete

A hand reaches out from between
folds of a flower smeared dress
nails, mud ingrained,
are flecked with pocks of dusky pink varnish

a wobbly wooden chair
planted on the long haired lawn
receives my tentative buttocks

and while I perch
clutching a glass of scrumpy
my great aunt Cicely
spins stories of lost relations
from fragments of memory
and wrapping it around me
like a woven shawl
I feel a sense of belonging
For the first time.

NO SUPPLICATIONS

no supplications up here
God told the hands
Reaching through holes in the floorboards
No wringing or wingeing
But winging yes wing it with buzz and flight
Trees have dreambodies
Their trunks lead to heaven
And their branches creep into sleep
So the floor boards which had been trees
Opened through imagining
And hands flapped free
Like white doves out of a numb fog
God smiled and said
Do I exist?
Answer your own prayers
And save yourselves
And the many winged hands
Beat a message through the world
Of healing spirits in every being
Just waiting to be heard
The freedom was enormous
But the devil was still thought to live [evil]
So did
and they all landed at Waterloo
To commence battle
Warriors against worriers
It was an anxious moment or two
But a good fight can release trapped energy
And life and death are two sides
of the same coin.

CURVES

Everyone needs a curve
Now and then
Too many straight lines
Cause narrowness.

I am squashed by the lifelessness
Of modern buildings - blank blocks
dumped to dissonate on dulled land

I imagine squads of depressed architects
In square offices
Lost in right angles
Unable to bend

Nature has no straight lines
Even the sea's horizon
Turns the slowest corner on earth.

TEA WITH A WALNUT TREE

The young walnut tree
Sitting next to me
Proffered a branch
So I took it and shook it
In a green and leafy way
Then sipped my earl grey

I invited walnut
For an after tea stroll
But it preferred to stay still
Citing roots as an excuse.

NUN

How crotchety
standing on an isthmus,
a nun knitting tufts of sheeps' wool
a blistered sister burnt by the sun
undone by smutty rumours
which hold water
like blocked drains
her black and white habit
falling apart and
grey in the face of
ordinary failings
and not much washing
so sending herself to penance alone
on a misty island.

She is annoyed that god never lent
a hand and frowns at a celtic cross
brooding on the beach,
with simpering waves lapping its bottom
then she's had enough and
howling turns pagan,
sows wild seeds
till soon there is a blaze of gorse
and a trail of hungry men.

The yellow flowers glow all year round
and smell of honey
and a colony grows
mothered by one
fathered by many
and a legend grows
of the loving magdalene
who turns no-one away.

THE WIND FROM MY SAILS

Thank you for taking
The wind from my sails
I'm floating in a
Sea of contentment
Admiring the daisies
on a lapping lawn
Watering my grave
Sense of self
With a dose of
salty irreverence

If a breeze comes along
I'll take the sails down
And just keep nosing
Along with the currents.

THE SINKING OF THE TEABAG

There the pallid and perforated skin
Browned off with life
Disappears beneath the boiling waves.
Like a lobster dunked
It yields its all
To an insensitive mug.

Born to be squashed by a teaspoon
Born to have its innermost feelings
leached away by a slurping mouth
born to end up in a mess by the sink

Spare a thought for the teabag.